101 EASTER JOKES FOR KIDS

BY: MIKKO MCGEE

Why did the Easter Bunny go to the beauty salon?

To get eggs-tensions in his hare.

What do you call a rabbit with fleas?

Bugs Bunny!

What did the rabbits do after their wedding?

They went on a bunnymoon!

What do you call a movie about a baby hen?

A chick flick!

Did you hear about the 500 hares that escaped from the zoo?

Police are combing the area!

What did the tree say to spring?

What a re-leaf!

What do you call a bunny with a dictionary in his pocket?

A smarty pants!

Knock, knock!
Who's there?
Alma.
Alma who?

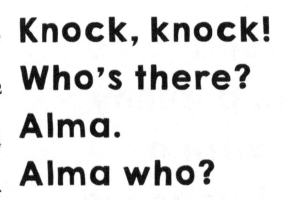 Alma Easter candy is gone. Can I have some more?

What day does an Easter egg hate the most?

Fry-day!

What kind of jewelry does the Easter Bunny wear?

14 carrot gold!

What is a duck's favorite game to play?

Billiards!

Why was the
little girl sad
after the
race?

Because an
egg beater!

What is the Easter Bunny's favorite state capital?

Albunny, New York!

What do you get when you cross a rabbit's foot with poison ivy?

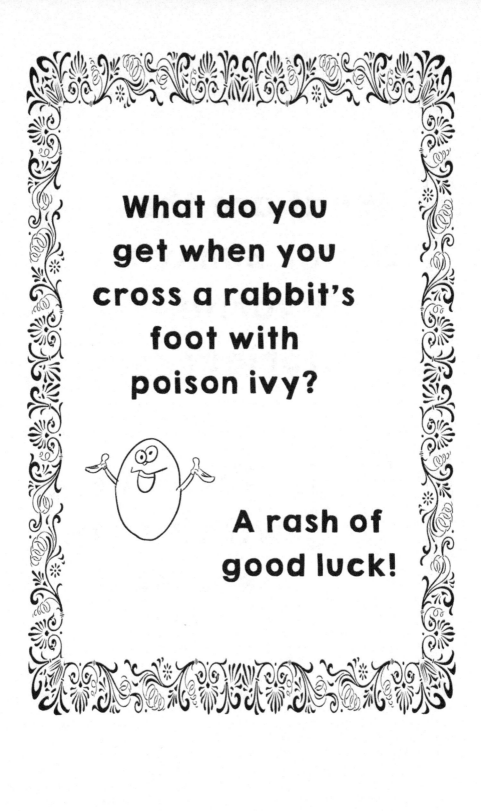

A rash of good luck!

What are the Easter Bunny's favorite stories?

The ones with hoppy endings!

What
happened to
the egg when it
was tickled?

It cracked
up!

What do you
get if you cross
an elephant
with a rabbit?

An elephant
who never
forgets to eat
his carrots!

What do you call ten rabbits marching backwards?

A receding hareline!

Why won't Easter eggs go out at night?

They don't want to get beat up!

How long does the spring duck like to party?

Around the cluck!

What's the Easter Bunny's favorite type of story?

A cotton tale!

Where does Dracula keep his Easter candy?

His Easter casket!

Why did the Easter Bunny have to fire the duck?

He kept quacking the eggs!

How do you catch a unique rabbit?

Unique up on it!

What do you call a forgetful rabbit?

A hare-brain!

What do you
get if you
take your
rabbits to
Arizona for
the summer?

Hot cross
bunnies!

How do you know that carrots are good for your eyes?

There are no rabbits with glasses!

How does the
Easter Bunny
keep his fur in
place?

With hare
spray!

What is the Easter Bunny's favorite dance?

The bunny hop!

What is the Easter Bunny's favorite sport?

Basket-ball!

What do you call the Easter Bunny the day after Easter?

Tired!

What did the eggs do when the light turned green?

They egg-cellerated!

How does an Easter chicken bake a cake?

From scratch!

What's a chicken farmer's favorite car?

A coupe!

Why did the
Easter Bunny
get fired from
the chocolate
factory?

He was
always taking
his sweet
time!

Why is the letter 'A' like a flower?

A 'B' comes after it!

What does the Easter Bunny get for making a basket?

Two points!

What happened
to the Easter
Bunny after he
misbehaved at
school?

He was
eggspelled!

Why are people always tired in April?

Because they just finished a march!

What sport are the eggs good at?

Running!

Knock, knock!
Who's there?
Sherwood.
Sherwood who?

Sherwood like to have an Easter basket like yours!

What type of movie is about waterfowl?

A duckumentary!

What do you call a rabbit with the sniffles?

A runny bunny!

How does the Easter Bunny travel?

By hare plane!

What did the rabbit say to the carrot?

It's been nice gnawing you!

Why do we paint Easter eggs?

Because it's too hard to wallpaper them!

What do you get if you cross a bee and a rabbit?

A honey bunny!

What is the Easter Bunny's favorite type of music?

Hip hop!

Why doesn't the
Easter Bunny
get candy at
the movie
theater?

They're always
raisinette!

What happened to the man who swallowed the food coloring?

He felt like he dyed a little inside.

What season is it when you are on a trampoline?

Spring-time!

What's long and stylish and full of kittens?

The Easter Purr-ade!

Where does the Easter Bunny go when he needs a new tail?

The re-tail store!

What would you
get if you
crossed the
Easter Bunny
with a famous
French general?

Napoleon
Bunnyparte!

What do you call a bunny with a large brain?

An egghead!

Why did the Easter Bunny cross the road?

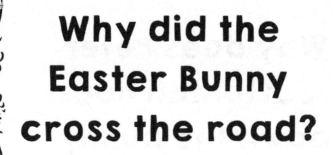

Because the chicken had his eggs!

Why does Peter Cottontail hop down the bunny trail?

Because he is too young to drive!

Why shouldn't you tell an Easter egg a joke?

It might crack up!

How does the Easter Bunny stay fit?

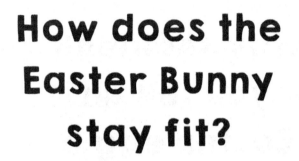

Eggs-ercise!

Why did the Easter egg hide?

He was a little chicken!

What happened
when the Easter
Bunny met the
rabbit of his
dreams?

They both
lived hoppily
ever after!

Where does the Easter Bunny like to eat breakfast?

IHOP!

What kind of beans grow in the Easter Bunny's garden?

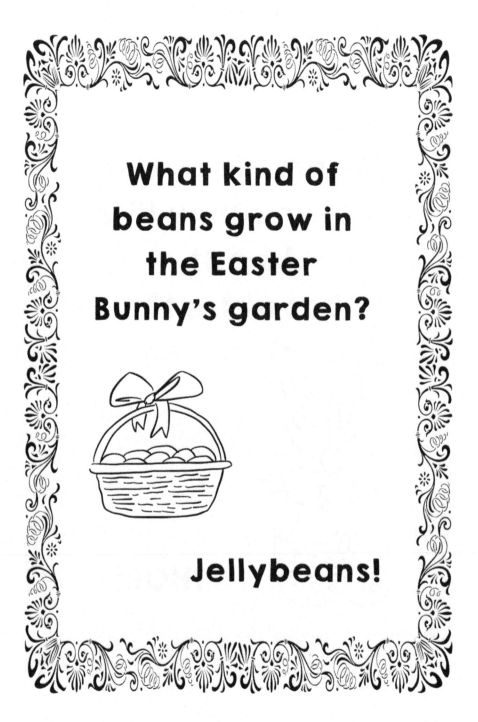

Jellybeans!

What did the
Easter egg say
to the other
Easter egg?

Have you
heard any
good yolks
today?

Why is the bunny the luckiest animal?

Because it has four rabbits' feet!

Why did the
woman buy the
baby chick
instead of a
baby duck?

Because it was
was a little
cheaper!

What do you get when you cross a bunny with an onion?

A bunion!

What did the bunny want to do when he grew up?

Join the Hare Force!

How did Antonio like working on the rabbit farm?

He said it was a hare raising experience!

How many
Easter eggs can
you put in an
empty basket?

One. After
that it's not
empty any
more!

What does a bunny use when it goes swimming?

A hare-net!

How do some
bunnies
commute to
work?

The Rabbit
Transit!

Where does the Easter Bunny get his eggs?

Eggplants!

How do you
know the Easter
Bunny liked his
trip?

Because he
said it was
egg-cellent!

What do you call a rabbit that tells good jokes?

A funny bunny!

How does the Easter Bunny keep his fur neat?

With a hare brush!

How does a rabbit throw a tantrum?

He gets hopping mad!

What did the chicken win at the contest?

A free range rover.

How do you know if a gardener is good at his job?

He springs into action!

What kind of duck can't keep his eyes closed?

A Peking duck.

What is the best way to send a letter to the Easter Bunny?

Hare mail!

What is the difference between a crazy bunny and a counterfeit bank note?

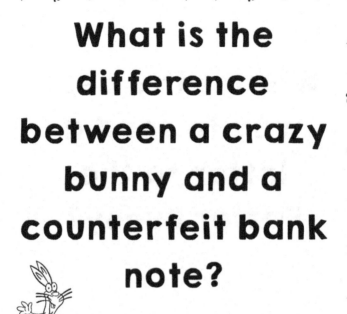

One is bad money and the other is a mad bunny!

How does Shrek like his eggs?

Ogre easy!

What do you call a mischievous egg?

A practical yolker !

What has big
ears, brings
Easter candy,
and goes
Hippity-BOOM!
Hippity-BOOM!
Hippity-BOOM!?

 The Easter
Elephant!

What do you call an egg from outer space?

An egg-stra terrestial!

How did the Easter Bunny dry himself after he got caught in the rain?

A hare dryer!

What does the Easter Bunny say when he burps?

Eggs-cuse me!

How can you tell where the Easter Bunny has been?

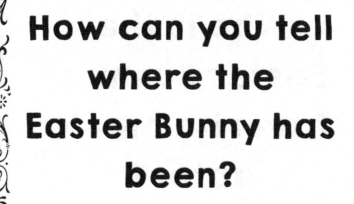

Eggs mark the spot!

Who is the Easter Bunny's favorite movie actor?

Rabbit De Niro!

What do you call a sleepy Easter egg?

Egg-zosted!

What do you get if you cross a hen with a dog?

Pooched eggs!

Where do you find information about eggs?

In the hen-cyclopedia!

Knock, knock!
Who's there?
Wendy.
Wendy who?

Wendy Easter
Bunny coming?

How is the Easter Bunny like LeBron James?

They're both famous for stuffing baskets!

How does
Easter end?

With an 'R'!

Made in the USA
Coppell, TX
11 March 2020